House Rules

House Rules

A tired parent's guide to chores, bedtime,
and other parenting trials

Alyssa Hoyt
Illustrated by Rachel Dietz

Published by Raindrop Books, 2020
www.reachingtowardstars.wordpress.com

Print ISBN 978-1-7358659-0-4

Ebook ISBN 978-1-7358659-1-1

Contents

House Rules

This book is the brainchild of a mom at her wit's end. My five kids were not meeting my expectations, and it seemed like no matter how many times I explained what needed to be done for simple jobs, the tasks were not adequately completed. You would think that after years of teaching how to do things like eat, brush teeth, and sit in a chair, my kids would know how to do those tasks. Alas, I had to write a book to help them out. Now they all know how to eat.

Please note that the expectations for my children may not be your expectations. My intent is not to offend but to entertain. Feel free to amend and modify our family's rules to meet your own. It's all for fun.

Thanks for the inspiration: Caden, Spencer, Shack, Micah and Emerson. This book is for you.

Throughout the book, you may find yourself curious about why we do things the way we do. To satisfy your curiosity, I've included a bit about our family at the end of the book.

While this book is somewhat tongue-in-cheek, feel free to make it required reading for your kids, too. I was fed up with my kids' lack of cooperation and made the handwritten version of the book mandatory reading.

Code of Conduct

Let it be known that until each member of our family is able to complete the tasks described herein, being asked only once to do said task, this Code of Conduct shall be the only reading material allowed except for school-related tasks for that person.

This includes reading for pleasure, reading instructions for games, reading cards, boards, or other items relating to games, reading information on the computer, reading what you type into a search engine, reading names of songs, or reading anything not required for tasks described herein or homework.

Bedroom

For six years, we lived in a 1,000-square-foot manufactured home. Before that, we were in a 30' travel trailer for a year. Living in smaller spaces and with less stuff has helped us streamline some systems and has influenced how we do things.

In our house, the bedrooms are used for sleeping and privacy (changing clothes). Most of our family's time is spent in community areas, and the toys are kept in community areas. This helps bedrooms stay (relatively) clean and makes the mess in a bedroom the responsibility of its occupant(s), not a sibling who was playing in there.

Getting changed

1. Take the clothes off your body that you're not going to wear anymore.
2. If an item of clothing you were wearing is dirty, it goes in the laundry basket. All the way in the laundry basket.
3. If it is clean, fold it and put it away. At least put it away, even if it doesn't get folded. And it needs to be put away, even if you're going to wear it again soon.
4. TIP: Socks and undies are always dirty and need to go in the laundry. They also need to be changed on a regular basis. More often than monthly. Or weekly. Daily would be nice.

TIP: Any other items: If you only wore it for 5 minutes, it is probably clean. If you played outside in it, it is probably dirty. If you only slept in it, it is probably clean. If you slept in it after wearing and sleeping in it for the last three days, it is dirty. If it passes the look and smell tests, it is probably clean and can be put away. Unless it has been on your body for three days. Then it is dirty, even if you don't think it looks or smells bad. Trust me.

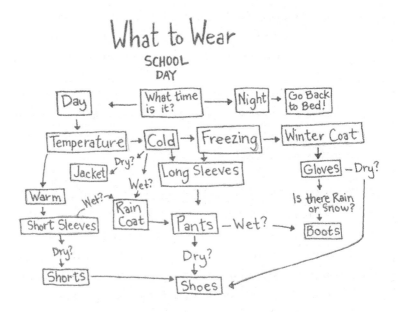

What to Wear
SCHOOL DAY

Deciding on clothes for the day: school days

1. Look out the window. Is it dark? Go to step two. Is it raining? See step three. Is there white stuff on the ground? Please go to step four. None of the above? Step five.
2. Dark: Either you need to go back to bed, or it is winter. If it is winter, it is probably cold. A long sleeved shirt and long pants would be appropriate.
3. Raining: You might consider wearing long pants and a warm shirt. You might also consider grabbing a raincoat on your way out.
4. White stuff = snow or frost. Either way, it is cold outside. Please wear long pants and a warm shirt. Your teachers get concerned when you wear shorts on days like today and they mention it to your mother, who assures them that you do indeed have sufficient warm clothes in your bedroom but that you choose to freeze instead.
5. Is it actually sunny? Wear whatever you want, because I know you're going to pick this option no matter what the weather: shorts and a T-shirt year-round.
6. Putting school clothes on over your pajamas does not count as getting dressed for school.

Deciding on clothes for the day: non-school days

- If it is a weekend/vacation day and we're not going out, wear whatever you want. Play clothes would be a great option.
- If it is a weekend/vacation day and we're going somewhere, please look presentable. This means no holes (other than the arm, head, and leg holes) and no stains. Small holes are still holes. Paint is a stain, even if your brother painted a spot your favorite shirt to get back at you for wearing his shirt one day. Collared shirts may be required if we're seeing grandparents, but I am somewhat flexible on this as long as the clothes you want to wear are actually clean and meet the previous requirements (no holes/stains).
- If we are going out to dinner or some other nice place, an old T-shirt and athletic shorts do not count as nice clothes, even if they don't have holes or stains.

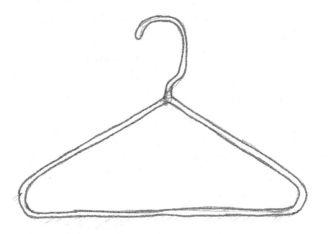

Storing clean clothes

1. Take clothes off the floor/off your bed/out of the laundry basket/etc.
2. Fold clothes that go in drawers (socks and undies don't have to be folded). Clothes that need to be hung go on neatly on a hanger, then put the hanger on the rod in the closet.
3. Put folded clothes into the drawer. Not back on your bed or in the laundry basket.
4. Repeat until all your clothes are put away.
5. If you get an item from the sorted laundry that does not belong to you, please put it on that person's bed or where it belongs. It does not go back into the laundry, or in the middle of the floor, or on the ceiling fan.

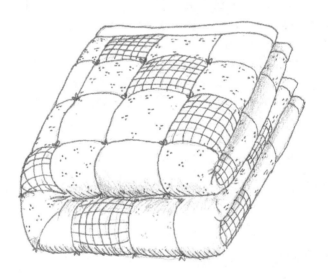

Tidy bed in the morning

1. No clothes on the bed. This includes putting them under the blankets (spread out flat so I can't see them) or stuffing in your pillowcase. Putting them away is actually less work than hiding them.
2. Blankets need to be neat.
3. Stuffed animals need to be neat.

Cleaning off the dresser

- If it is trash, put it in the trash can.
- If it is art and you want to keep it, display it neatly. If you don't want to keep it, recycle it or throw it away.
- If it is a toy, put it away.
- If it is someone else's, return it.
- If it is a book that does not belong to you and you're not in the middle of reading it, put it on the community bookshelf.
- If it belongs inside the dresser, put it there.
- If there is anything left that needs to be removed, do it. If you need help finding homes for things, ask a parent.
- It is OK to have a few things out for display or enjoyment. Please make them look nice.

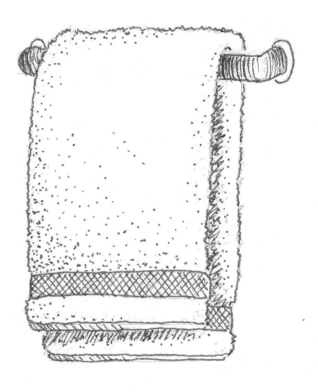

Using the bathroom

Our family is different from most in that we use "toilet cloths" instead of toilet paper at our house. We have a basket near each toilet for clean cloths, and a lidded bin for dirty ones. As a parent, I love having a large supply of cleaning rags readily available. As a consumer of the cloths, I feel much cleaner using actual cloth than toilet paper. I don't know if it is better for the environment or not (it certainly uses energy to wash and dry them), but I really like using them. Having used and washed cloth diapers for some of my kids, it seemed a natural transition. And we do put TP out for guests.

Peeing

1. Boys: If you're going to stand, put the seat up to pee. When you're done, put it back down. Your future spouse will think you're amazing.
2. Everyone: if you get urine anywhere except for inside the toilet, wipe it up. Immediately.
3. Flush.
4. WASH YOUR HANDS. With soap. See "handwashing."

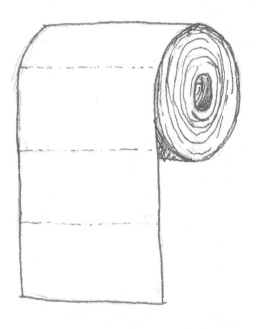

Pooping

1. When you're done with your business, flush. If it doesn't go down, stay in the bathroom. Either try flushing again, or plunge the toilet. If the toilet is close to overflowing, turn the water valve off so the bathroom doesn't flood.

2. Check to make sure the toilet cloth(s) you used made it into the dirty bin. Yes? Great. Thanks. No? Use another toilet cloth (a clean one) to pick it up and deposit it into the bin. Not sure if your cloth made it in the bin? If there are any cloths on the floor next to the bin, assume they are yours and that they are dirty. Pick it up using a clean cloth and put it in the bin.

3. If you wipe boogers on the wall of the bathroom while you're sitting there picking your nose (is going to the bathroom really that boring?), clean them up. Now. Why didn't you wipe them on a toilet cloth in the first place? See "washing walls" if you decide to leave the boogers on the wall.

4. OK - double check: Toilet flushed? Dirty cloths in the bin? Walls clean?

5. If those things are done, wash your hands. With soap. See "handwashing."

6. If any poop gets on the seat of the toilet, clean it up.

Bathing/Showering

1. Clothes off, water on. Close the door if you want privacy and a warm bathroom when you get out.
2. Fan on.
3. Get in the shower.
4. Get all wet, including your hair. This is important for the next steps.
5. Using soap or shampoo, wash your hair, then rinse it out.
6. Do the same with conditioner if you'd like.
7. Using soap, wash your entire body. If there is exposed skin, wash it. Behind your knees? Yes. Armpits? Yes. Face? Yes. Behind your ears? Yes. In between toes? Yes. Rear end? Yes. Penis? Yes. If you're not circumcised, it is a good idea to retract the foreskin and rinse the tip - no soap needed there. Vulva? Yes. Inside your nose? No. Got everything? Put the soap away.
8. NOTE: Steps #5 and #7 are vital steps in this process. It is not a shower/bath if those steps did not happen.
9. Rinse off all the soap.
10. Turn the water off. This is also an important step.
11. Dry off using a towel or a robe. Shaking like a dog will not get you dry enough.
12. Put the towel away. This means hanging it on a towel rack or on a hook.
13. Take care of the clothes you wore into the bathroom. Clean? See "putting clean clothes away." Dirty? See "getting changed."

Handwashing

1. Even if your hands look clean, you should still wash
    them occasionally, as well as every time you use the
    bathroom, come home from school, and before you
    eat. Once a week is not occasional enough.
2. Turn the water on. Hot water is good; warm water
    is acceptable, cold water is better than nothing.
3. Get your hands wet.
4. Put soap on your hands. If the liquid soap is empty,
    use bar soap. Wiping one hand once over the top of
    the bar soap is not enough contact to get soap on
    your hands. Squirting liquid soap into your hand
    and immediately rinsing it off in the water, then
    rubbing your hands together is also an insufficient
    amount of soap. A sufficient amount of soap is
    required for this activity to qualify as
    "handwashing."
5. Rub soapy hands together, covering all the surfaces
    with suds. That includes all of your fingers, in
    between your fingers, and the back of your hands.
    Because I've seen you wipe your nose on the back
    of your hand, I know it's dirty.
6. Rinse off your hands in the sink under running
    water.
7. Dry your hands on a towel. Place the towel back on
    the rack if it comes off while you are drying your
    hands.

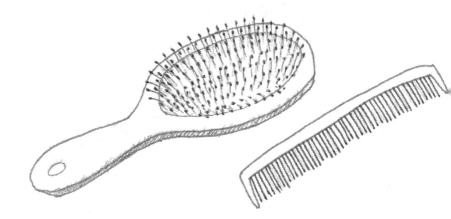

Brushing hair

1. Find your brush or comb. In our house, it should be in the drawer in the bathroom. If it is not, look in your bedroom, your backpack, the living room, next to the computer, under your pillow, or on the stairs.*
2. Short hair: why are you even combing it? Isn't this the benefit of having short hair?
3. Long hair: Brush your hair away from your head. If it is really tangly, you can start midway down the length of your hair.
4. Continue brushing a section of hair until the brush or comb runs through without any resistance.
5. Move on to the next section of hair and repeat step four.
6. Repeat step five until all your hair is tangle-free.

*Speaking of looking for things, you'll notice that I give the same response for many things: "Did you look where it is supposed to go?"

Bathroom jobs

As many times as I have shown my kids how to actually do these jobs, it seemed like some of the essential aspects of them were always missed. Like actually getting something clean. Maybe they figured out that if they did a poor job and I had to show them how to do it, I actually did the job for them..... Having clear descriptions helped. A little bit.

Sink (quick wipe down)

1. Use vinegar spray to moisten the faucet and sink. If there are large things in the sink (rocks, for example, or clumps of hair, or toothbrushes), remove them first.
2. Wipe it with a cloth.
3. Rinse with water. Make sure to get all the dried toothpaste chunks down the drain. And the dirt bits that came off the rocks when you removed them.

Sink (deep clean)

1. This should be an easy job because every day this week, people have taken their turns to do a quick wipe down. Right? Anyone? Anyone?
2. Moisten the sink and faucet with spray.
3. Sprinkle baking soda thinly all over the sink.
4. Using a cloth, scrub all around the sink. If there are any stubbornly dirty spots, scrub them a little more.
5. Rinse the cloth off, and use it to help wipe down the sink with clean water.
6. Make sure all the baking soda gets washed down and there is no residue left on the sink or faucet. If there is, repeat steps four and five.

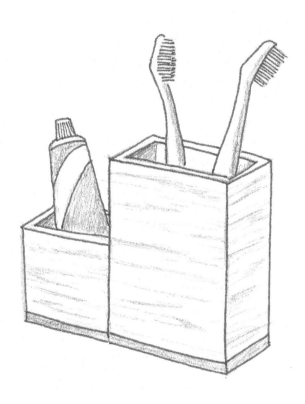

Counter

1. Put away all the stuff that is on the counter. The only things that should be on the counter are the jar of toothbrushes and soap dispensers. This does not include hair brushes, towels, toothpaste tubes or caps (and why are the caps never on the tubes?), used floss, hair bands, or Legos.

2. Use vinegar spray to moisten the counter, then wipe the surface clean with a cloth. Yes, even the dried-on toothpaste. You will need to move the toothbrush jar and the soap dispensers in order to get the whole counter clean because the counter does actually get dirty underneath things.

Mirror

1. Use vinegar spray to moisten, then wipe clean with a cloth.
2. Check your work. If the spots didn't go away or the mirror still looks dirty, do it again. If there are water streaks, wipe again with a dry cloth.

Inside toilet (daily)

1. Flush. Just to make sure.
2. Scrub bowl with brush.
3. Flush again.

Inside toilet (weekends)

1. Flush. Just to make sure.
2. Squirt toilet bowl cleaner all around the inside of the rim.
3. Scrub bowl with brush.
4. Flush again. Take a look inside the bowl. Does it look clean inside? If it doesn't, please scrub it again.

Outside toilet

1. Spray all outside surfaces of the toilet with vinegar spray. This means the lid, the back of the toilet, under the seat, on the seat, on the rim, and around the base. Yes, this is really gross. It would be less gross if you actually peed in the toilet every time.
2. Wipe it down with a cloth.

Floor around toilet

1. Move items out of the way. Toilet cloth bin? Trash? Rug? Toilet brush? Yes, yes, yes and yes!
2. Spray the floor with vinegar spray.
3. Wipe with a cloth.
4. Return items to where they belong.

After each bath job is complete, where does the dirty cloth need to go? That's right, in the dirty toilet cloth bin! If you miss, pick it up and put it in the bin.

Kitchen

Everyone in our house shares kitchen chores. During school (and often on the weekends and vacations), breakfast and breakfast cleanup is on your own. All my kids pack their own lunches and have since kindergarten. Dinner is our group meal, and everyone has responsibilities. All the kids take turns helping cook, and everyone has a dinner chore every night.

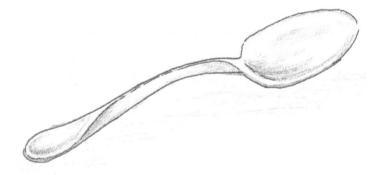

Cooking, part 1

1. Decide on the meal. If we had it for dinner the day before, you need to think of something else. Your choice needs to include at least two different colorful vegetables. French fries and ketchup do not count as two vegetables.

2. If we do not have the ingredients for what you want to make, you will need to choose something else, or make a substitution for something we do have. Just so you know, cumin is not an acceptable substitution for cinnamon when you're making cinnamon sugar. I know the words LOOK similar, but please smell it before you put it in.

3. Prepare the meal. It is OK to ask for help!

    a. If you're following a single recipe, please continue to step 4.

    b. If you're not following a recipe, or are making multiple recipes, start with the steps that take the longest. If you wait to roast the sweet potatoes until after you cook the pasta, you will have a slimy, luke-warm brick of pasta by the time the potatoes are done.

4. Prep your ingredients. Yes, I will help you chop the onions because I know that you close your eyes so they don't sting and I'd hate to have you chop your finger off. That makes dinner take longer.

Cooking, part 2

5. Once your ingredients are ready, you can actually start cooking! Unless the recipe specifies otherwise, please cook things on medium-ish heat. Too low, it won't cook. Too high, and the way we know dinner is ready is because the smoke alarm will go off and everyone will run outside for a fire drill.

6. Please cook the food until it is actually cooked but not overdone. Dipping noodles in boiling water does not cook them; leaving them in tepid water for 30 minutes doesn't either. Cooking them for 30 minutes in boiling water is too long and no one likes mush for dinner. If you're not sure how long to cook something, ask a parent or check the packaging.

7. Make sure there is water in your pot along with the vegetables, or pasta, or oatmeal. Or your teakettle, for that matter. It is amazing how hot a pot can get. Have you ever seen molten metal? Neither had I. And it is really hard to clean off the stove.

8. Clean up as you go: cutting boards, knives, prep bowls, etc. Wipe up spills as they happen.

9. Put away gadgets or appliances used.

10. Compost goes in the bin.

Setting the table

1. Set out hot pads, utensils, plates or bowls. Salt? Pepper? Candles or centerpiece? Putting out all of our plates and the entire flatware drawer isn't actually funny, even if you think it is. We're not formal here, so you don't have to lay out anything, just get it to the table. We'll figure it out from there. It actually makes serving a lot easier if all the plates are in one spot instead of at each person's seat.
2. Set out condiments and serving utensils.
3. Are we eating something messy or greasy? Put out napkins.
4. Before you put the hot food dishes on the table, please make sure there is adequate space for it on the table. Putting it on the tortilla bag melts the bag and melted plastic is really hard to clean off of a casserole dish.

Clearing the table

1. Everyone is responsible for his or her own dishes. And cups. And utensils. This means taking them off the table, scraping any scraps into the compost, rinsing it if needed, and loading everything into the dishwasher or hand washing it.
2. Put leftover food into containers, then into the fridge. Make a lunch container of leftovers for Dad if necessary.
3. Clear all dishes, condiments, hot pads, etc, putting things away as you go. If a dish is dirty but clean enough to go straight into the dishwasher without rinsing, please put it there instead of on the counter. The table should be empty when you're done clearing.
4. Wipe the table. If you just push the crumbs onto the floor, you'll need to sweep, too.

Doing dishes

1. All dishes from meal prep need to be washed or loaded into the dishwasher.
2. All dishes, pots, and pans from the meal need to be washed or loaded into the dishwasher. See "hand-washing dishes" if additional instructions are needed.
3. The sink should be empty and wiped down with strainers clean and dishwashing tools put away.
4. Run the garbage disposal if necessary. Check it first to make sure it is empty. If you run it with the chainmail scrubber in it, for example, it will get tiny pieces of metal chainmail stuck in the disposal and ruin the scrubber. Just sayin'.

Hand-washing dishes

1. While it is frustrating that not everything fits in the dishwasher every time, that is reality. We use baking sheets and large pots that sometimes won't fit in. Just deal with it. However, if a person intentionally makes a meal that uses lots of large dishes because they want to punish the person whose turn it is to do the dishes, the mealmaker can help hand-wash dishes that night.

2. In case this wasn't clear from the get-go, dishwashing happens in the sink, and all the water should stay there.

3. Rinse the dirty dish with hot water.

4. Squirt some dish soap onto the dish. One small squirt is usually enough. 10 pumps or a long stream from the bottle is excessive. It is sometimes more economical to fill a large dish or one side of the sink with soapy water to wash the dishes in.

5. Scrub the dishes with a cloth, sponge, or brush. Your choice.

6. Rinse the dishes in clean, hot water.

7. Check the item you just washed. Can you see food on it? It's not clean, please do it again. Can you feel scum or food bits on it with your finger? It's not clean, please do it again. Repeat steps 4-6 until the item is clean.

8. Either dry the dish yourself, set it on the drying rack, or ask someone to help you dry the dish. Then put it away.

Wrap up

1. You're the support person for the dish washer.
2. Wipe the counters and stovetop.
3. Dry and put away the hand-washed dishes. Snapping the dish washer with your towel while you're waiting for him/her to finish washing a dish will result in you washing and drying the rest of the dishes.
4. Make sure the dishwasher has detergent in it and gets started.
5. Hang towels up or put them in the wash when you're done.

Taking out the compost

1. Take out all the compost. If you waited too long and there is a plate of compost in addition to the regular bucket, you'll need to take that out, too.
2. Dump the compost in the compost bin outside. Not on the porch, not in the middle of the path, not on the cat, and not in your sibling's bicycle helmet.
3. Rinse the compost bucket out. I know it's nasty. It is nasty because no one ever does this step. If it is done every time, it would be less nasty.
4. Return the compost bucket to its spot under the sink. With the lid closed and sealed, please.

Snacks and lunch-making

1. Lunches and snacks need to include "growing food." Start with a fruit and a vegetable. Once you have that, add some protein and carbs.
2. Clean up after yourself. If you spill, wipe it up. If you drip, wipe it up. If you get it out, put it away. If you ask someone to leave something out for you, you need to put it away. If you can reach to get it down, you can reach to put it away, too.
3. Put your compost in the bin and close the lid securely.

Trash out

1. Tie the bag of trash so the top is closed.
2. Take the bag to the trash can by the street.
3. Put a new bag in the inside trash can, and put it under the sink.

Recycle out

1. Take the bin to the cart at the street and dump it out.
2. Glass goes in its own bin.
3. Return recycle bin to its place under the sink.

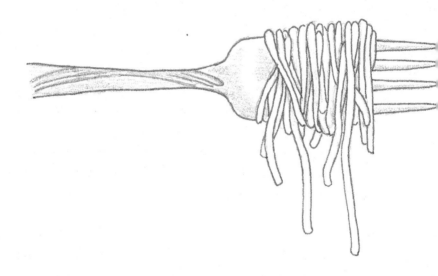

Eating

1. Sit in a chair or on the bench (see "sitting").
2. Put food on an eating utensil.
3. With your mouth over your plate or bowl, bring the food to your mouth. Open your mouth, insert utensil food end first.
4. Close mouth, remove utensil (leave the food), and keep mouth closed while chewing.
5. Swallow before inserting more food. Or laughing. Or talking.
6. Repeat.
7. You must eat your vegetables before you get more of the food you really like.
8. When the food on your plate is gone and you don't want more, the plate goes to the dishwasher. Licking your plate does not count as washing it, even if you can't see any more food particles. On second thought, just don't lick your plate in the first place.
9. If you're doing anything while eating that encourages an audience, you may be choosing to leave the table without the opportunity to finish the meal. Even if that audience is your own reflection in the kitchen window.

Cooking eggs

1. Preheat pan. "High" is likely to burn your eggs. Even if you're in a hurry to go to school, it won't cook them that much faster. "Low" is likely to leave them raw, at least in the time you have before you need to leave. Find some good middle ground.
2. Get out eggs and whatever seasonings you're going to use. Salt and pepper are good. The entire bottle of cumin is bad.
3. Add grease to the pan.
4. Decide if you're cooking scrambled eggs or fried eggs. Sometimes the fried eggs end up being scrambled eggs, so be flexible.
5. Crack eggs into the pan. Cracking them on the stove can lead to a raw egg on the stove.
6. Cook the eggs to your desired done-ness.
7. Put the eggs on a plate, or in a tortilla on a plate. Eating them out of the pan is bad manners. Eating them off the stove is gross. Please don't.

Making a sandwich

1. Decide what type of sandwich you're going to make. This will determine the next steps. Peanut butter and jam? Tuna fish? Egg salad? Ham and cheese? Rice and beans? Grilled cheese? The rice and beans option doesn't sound very good to me, but it's your sandwich.
2. Get out bread and fillings.
3. Put the bread on a plate. While step five is part of this process, for some reason it rarely gets done, so please use a plate to minimize the mess.
4. Put the filling on the bread, using an appropriate utensil. Fingers are not appropriate utensils for peanut butter, jam, tuna fish, or egg salad.
5. Clean up your mess, including wiping all the crumbs off the counter into the compost or trash, not onto the floor. Onto the floor is not cleaning up.
6. Enjoy your sandwich!

Pouring cereal, the two-year-old way

1. Placing a small bowl onto the floor, dump out the rest of the box of cereal into the bowl.
2. Pour the rest of the carton of milk over the cereal.
3. Move the bowl to the table, dripping milk and soggy cereal from the kitchen to the table.
4. Thoughtfully go back to the kitchen and use a towel to spread the milk and cereal all over the kitchen. Take the dripping towel down the hall, up the stairs, and around the corner to the washing machine.
5. Get a spoon.
6. Eat breakfast.

Pouring cereal, the 13-year-old way

1. Get out a bowl. Not a mixing bowl, although I am sure you could finish that amount of cereal.
2. Get out three boxes of cereal and a full gallon of milk.
3. Have a bowl of cereal #1.
4. Have a bowl of cereal #2.
5. Have a bowl of cereal #3.
6. Have a bowl of all three mixed together, thoughtfully leaving ⅓ of a serving of each type of cereal in the box for the rest of the family.
7. Drink milk directly out of the jug, thoughtfully leaving two tablespoons to dampen the 14 pieces of cereal left in the boxes.
8. Thoughtfully put the boxes away in the pantry, which leaves Mom to assume that there is enough cereal for everyone to have breakfast that day.

Getting things out of the fridge

1. Before opening the fridge, decide what it is you want to remove from the fridge.
2. Open the fridge and locate the item you are looking for.
3. Make sure there is a clear path of exit from the location of the item to the edge of the shelf. For example, if you want the egg carton and there is a jar of salsa in front of it, move the salsa out of the way so it doesn't get knocked onto the floor.
4. If the item you are removing from the fridge has a lid, either a) lift the item by the sides or bottom, or b) make sure the lid is securely attached before lifting the item by the lid. Because jarred minced garlic, when dropped, explodes out of the top of the jar and covers the floor, chairs, counter, cabinet doors, table, and gets into the heating vents.
5. Securely holding the item you are removing, take the item out of the fridge and close the fridge doors.
6. Repeat steps 1 - 5 for all the items you would like to get out of the fridge.

Living

I have found that there are some skills that I assumed my kids learned along the way that they actually didn't pick up on. It is ironic to me that children don't need to be taught how to yell at each other, pretend that a stick is a gun, or make messes, but it takes a monumental amount of effort to help them learn how to speak kindly, play peacefully, and clean up after themselves.

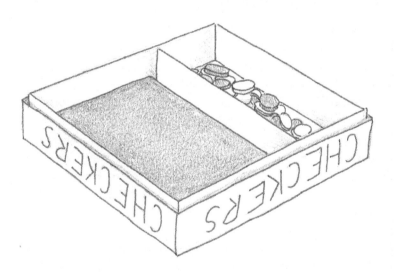

Cleaning up

- Clean up after yourself. If you participated in an activity that involved others, stay and help clean up until the activity is completely put away.
- "Put away" means putting an item in the place it belongs.
- It is especially nice if the space you used is left cleaner than how you found it.

Saying please

- Please really is a magic word. Saying it magically makes things happen for you!
- Adults will tend to respect you if you are polite and use words like "please," "thank you," and "excuse me." While being a kid in an adult world can be really frustrating at times, using these words will get you a long way.
- Demanding something (either an item or a service) from someone is generally not a good strategy. If the person says no, begging won't help you get what you want.
- Exceptions to the please rule include:
  a. Bodily violence. You don't have to say please if someone is tickling, strangling, punching, hitting, biting, or otherwise abusing you.
  b. Protection. If you are protecting someone else from bodily violence or otherwise unwanted behaviors, you do not have to say please.

Consent

- You are in charge of your own body and choices. And you are not in charge of anyone else's body or choices.
- Ask permission before doing things to other people.
- No means no.
- You ALWAYS have the ability to say no to someone who wants you to do something, and they need to respect that. There may be consequences, but you always have the choice. If you choose to say no to Mom when she asks you to do your chores, there WILL be consequences. Negative ones. But you do have the choice. If your friends or romantic partner don't respect your right to say no, find new friends or a new partner.
- Be clear in your communication. If you're laughing while someone is teasing you, you may be communicating to them that you like it. If you say "Stop!" but continue wrestling, the other person will be confused and might think you're giving consent to continue the activity.

Conflict resolution

- We all experience conflict with others. How we deal with it is important. The number one thing to remember is that if you don't communicate, nothing will be resolved.
- I can't teach you how to solve all your problems. I can only give you tools to use during times of conflict. I trust that you will use them when you need them.
- It is difficult to resolve conflict when emotions are high. If you need to, take time to cool off.
- Blame does not resolve conflict. Use the nonviolent communication format to communicate how you're feeling, what your needs are, and how the other person can help resolve the conflict: "When I see/hear/observe you _____, I feel _____. I need _____. Please _____." *
- The tone and volume of your words communicates just as much as the language you use. Consider how you are saying your words.
- Body language communicates just as much as words. Aggressive posture or invading someone's space suggests dominance and will likely increase the conflict.
- We don't communicate with violence. It is not a tool available to you in your toolbox.
- Listen. Conflict resolution is a two-way street. Hear the other person's perspective before jumping to conclusions about their intentions.

* Please visit cnvc.org for more information.

Sitting

1. Find a place to sit that is not occupied by another human being. If it is occupied, ask that human's permission before sitting on top of them. Not everyone likes being sat upon.

2. If the place you want to sit has been recently vacated by another human being, make sure they are not returning before taking their spot. And if you pushed them out of their seat so you could sit there, you may not sit there.

3. Once you get to your place of rest, your rear end should be touching the seat of the object, the seat should be right side up, and it should have as much contact with the ground as it was designed for. Thus, sitting on the back of a chair is not safe; nor is sitting on the chair while it is upside down; nor is balancing on a chair's two rear legs.

4. If sitting is happening at a table while you're eating, then your knees should be beneath the table. Your feet should be there, too. Your face should be somewhere in the vicinity of your own plate. Not your neighbor's plate. Or their lap.

5. If sitting is happening on the floor, please make sure that your most pleasant side is up. Your buttocks shouldn't be the highest point of your body, nor should they be pointing at me. And please make sure that clothes are covering all the parts of your body that you don't want me to see.

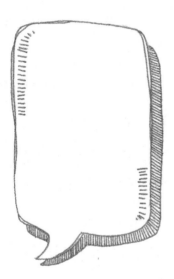
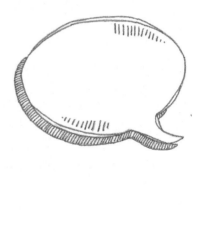

Having a conversation

1. If you already know the person, you should have something in common. School, a shared place where you've been, some kind of shared experience... I am sure you can think of something. Talk about that.

2. If you don't know the person, ask them questions. About themselves. That aren't too personal. Asking something like, "How's puberty going?" is not a good way to start a conversation (yes, I have had a child ask that). We call those conversation killers at our house.

3. Once you find something you have in common, talk about that. And then find something else you have in common, because talking about Legos every time you talk to someone gets old after a while.

4. Eye contact is helpful, but not essential. If prolonged eye contact makes you uncomfortable, look at the person for a couple seconds, then find something else to look at for a while. Just check in with their eyes every now and then. It helps them feel like you're listening.

Closing doors

1. Go through the door you want to close. This is an important step, because some people like to hang out in the opening of the door that needs to be closed. This especially seems to happen on cold days at exterior doors.

2. Grasp the handle of the door, and gently but firmly close the door behind you. Did you hear a loud slam? That was too hard. Did the entire house shake as you closed the door? Also too hard. Did the door open again after you closed it? Either you closed it on the person following you, or you need to try again, a little bit harder this time. Was there a loud scream as you closed the door? Someone's fingers are stuck, please open the door again. And run to get the ice pack.

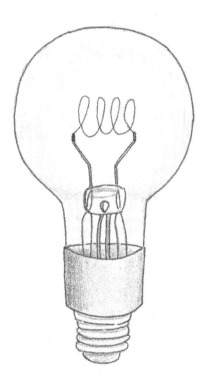

Using a light switch

1. When you go into a room and it is dark, use the light switch to turn on the light. If the room is already light because it is daytime, you do not need to turn the light on.
2. When you are leaving the room, use the light switch to turn the light off. This step is mandatory, unless there is an exception. See step three.
3. The only exception to the second step of this rule is if there is someone else in the room who needs the light on. Then the light needs to be left on.

Going up stairs

1. Take one foot and lift it up onto the first step, holding the handrail for support if desired.
2. Shift your weight to this foot.
3. Lift the second foot up, pass the first step that foot #1 is on, and place it on the second step.
4. Shift your weight to the second foot.
5. Repeat, alternating steps until you reach the top.
6. Unsuccessful but creative ways I have seen people attempt to climb stairs:
   a. Putting a large box over your entire body and jumping up the stairs.
   b. Putting your body into a large box and attempting to hop up the stairs. Backwards. This may result in a bloody nose at the bottom of the stairs.
   c. Holding your heels to your bottom and walking up the stairs on your knees.
   d. Hopping on one foot while skipping every other step.
   e. Doing jump squats up the stairs. Skipping one at a time was successful. Trying to skip two resulted in bruised shins.
7. Caution should be exercised when going up stairs to ensure that you are not involved in a collision with people trying to slide, jump, roll, or fly down the stairs.

Going down stairs

1. Reverse the process of going up stairs. I recommend bending your knees. Not bending your knees results in a comical but not very safe path of descent.

Other chores

Since there weren't enough chores at our house already.

Washing dirty laundry

1. Gather the dirty laundry. At our house, this includes the basket from the boys' room, the basket in the girls' room, Mom and Dad's basket, and anything on top of the washer.
2. Some people like to sort laundry by color, texture, weight of material, level of filth, etc. If you are helping someone who likes to sort laundry this way, please do it their way. At our house, clothes only fall into two categories: clean or dirty. If it is dirty, it goes in the basket. If it is clean, it gets put away.
3. Put the dirty laundry into the washing machine.
4. Add laundry detergent using the cup in the top of the lid. Please do not guess by just pouring the detergent into the washer. You will guess wrong. If you are not sure how to do this, please ask.
5. Turn on the washer.
6. Most of the time, the cycle will be normal, high spin, and cold water. Ask me about exceptions. You don't need to cycle through all the options just to hear the machine beep. Just leave it where it was.
7. Make sure the door is closed, and push start. Pushing start is important; otherwise the clothes don't get clean. Then when you go to put the clothes in the dryer, the dirty clothes just get tumbled around and put back in your drawer dirty. Gross.

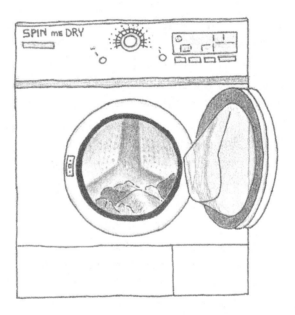

Drying laundry, option one

1. Look out the window to evaluate the weather. Is it sunny and warm-ish? Does it look like it might rain today? Don't get too distracted and start thinking about jumping on the trampoline, we're doing laundry here.

2. If the weather looks like it would not dry laundry (ie cloudy or rainy), proceed to step three. If the weather looks like it could dry laundry, please go to "Drying laundry, option two."

3. Open the dryer door and make sure the last person emptied the lint trap. If they did, great! If they didn't, you will need to scrape off the lint from the last load and put it in the trash can, then replace the lint trap.

4. Take the laundry out of the washer.

5. Put the laundry into the dryer.

6. Turn the dryer on.

7. Set the dryer to the appropriate drying cycle (auto is good).

8. Push start.

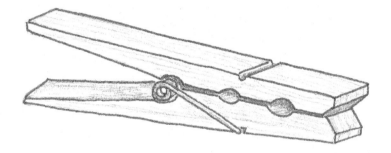

Drying laundry, option two

1. See step one for option one of "Drying laundry." If the weather looks like it could dry clothes (i.e. no rain), you can dry the laundry on the clothesline outside. Proceed to step two here.

2. Put the clean and wet laundry from the washer into the laundry basket. Make sure the clothes you're taking out of the washer actually got washed. If they are dry, they are probably still dirty because the person who loaded them forgot to start the washer.

3. Take the laundry basket outside. Make sure to grab clothespins.

4. Take each item from the basket and hang them on the line so they are spread out. I find it nice to hang the big, easy-to-hang things first. Hang shirts by the bottom, putting a clip on each end. Hang pants by the cuffs. Overlapping the clothes a tiny bit at each end and pinning them up together uses fewer clothespins. Leaving socks crumpled up results in crunchy balls of fabric.

5. Hang everything you can. If it doesn't all fit, spread the remaining items out on the edge of the basket, or put them in the dryer for a few minutes.

6. Let the laundry get all the way dry. This usually takes a few hours.

7. Take the laundry down. Collect the clothespins and put the laundry back in the basket, then take it upstairs. You may want to shake items outside to get rid of any insects, spiders, or frogs that decided to take up residence in your underwear.

Sorting clean laundry

1. If needed, get the laundry out of the dryer.
2. Sort everyone's clothes, as well as towels, washcloths, etc. to the appropriate place.
3. Put your own clothes away.
4. Put community items away: hats, gloves, bath towels, kitchen towels, napkins, hot pads, etc.
5. Put Mom's and Dad's things on their bed.

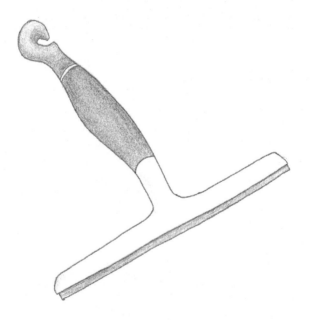

Washing windows

1. Gather supplies: squeegee, cloths, window spray, scraper if necessary.
2. Generously spray the window, or use a wet cloth to get the window wet.
3. Wipe the entire window with the cloth, scrubbing hard on stubborn spots. Scrape those spots if needed.
4. Use the squeegee to wipe all the moisture off the window, starting at the top corner and overlapping swaths. Dry the squeegee with a cloth after every pass. Wipe up any liquid that ends up on the windowsill.
5. Evaluate your work. If it looks worse now than when you started, do it again. If you already did it again and it looks even worse, it's time to ask for help.
6. Put the cleaning tools away.

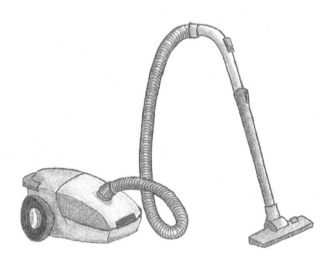

Vacuuming

1. Pick everything up off the floor of the area if that is not already done. You can leave large furniture in place.
2. Get the vacuum out. Pull the cord out to the yellow tape and plug it in. Pulling it out as far as it goes is not good for the cord. Other people might have vacuums with cords that wind up. Unwind the cord all the way. Empty the dirt cup if needed.
3. Using parallel swaths, vacuum the entire carpeted surface of the room. If the edges need attention, disconnect the hose and use the attachments.
4. Vacuums are not picky about whether they suck up dirt, dog hair, Legos, or vacuum cords, so please keep the cord out of the path of the vacuum.
5. Unplug, retract or wind the cord, and put the vacuum away.

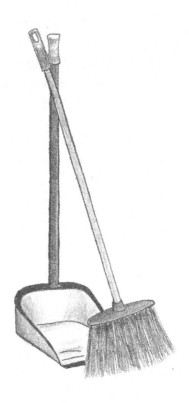

Sweeping

1. Sweeping is very similar to vacuuming, but sucks a bit less.
2. Pick up everything off the floor of the area where you're going to sweep if that is not already done.
3. Using a pulling motion, move the broom along the floor without launching dirt and dust into the air.
4. As you go across a room, get into all the nooks and crannies that you can. Go all the way to the edge of the wall. Be methodical about your sweeping pattern so you get the entire surface of the floor. Sweeping a room with a star shape to get things into the middle of the room will make a nice pattern, but not a clean floor.
5. After sweeping the entire room, you should be able to sweep the dirt into a manageable pile. Sweep this pile into the dustpan (make sure you get it all; it will take a few brushes with the broom) and deposit the contents into the trash.

Dusting

1. Gather supplies: either spray and a dry cloth or a damp cloth.
2. Remove any items that are on the surface which you are about to dust. Yes, I realize that if the statue/priceless vase/book is always on the shelf there won't be dust under it. This is not about being logical, it is about being thorough and knowing how to do it right.
3. Spray the surface and wipe it clean. Look at your cloth. See how nasty that is? That's all dust that used to be floating around in the air you have been breathing. Doesn't that make you feel better?
4. If there are stripes of clean areas and dirty areas, wipe the surface again until it is all clean.
5. Replace the statue/priceless vase/book CAREFULLY and move on to the next dusty place.

In an attempt to keep the inside of our house a little bit cleaner, we have a shoes-off rule. We have a porch and rack to place shoes on. The racks are usually empty, but at least they are there.

Shoes

1. Remove your shoes outside. That does not mean in the mud room, or upstairs in your bedroom, or outside after you come in and go to the bathroom. It means to take them off outside before you come in the house.
2. Place your shoes somewhere they will not get tripped over. Placing your shoes anywhere people usually walk is a place where they shouldn't be. This includes the doormat, which is right in front of the door. Don't put your shoes there.

Feeding the dog/cat/fish/hamster/iguana....

1. If it is time for the animal to be fed, the bowl is empty, and the animal is begging for food, assume no one has done the job yet.
2. Get the food out.
3. Put the appropriate amount in the bowl. The entire bag is not an appropriate amount. Less than that.
4. Put the food away when you're done. If you don't, one of two things will happen: we won't need to feed the dog for a week because it just ate the entire bag, or we just announced to all the ants and rodents in the area that there is a free buffet at our house.

Washing walls

1. Gather supplies: vinegar spray and cloths or a damp cloth. Sometimes a Magic Eraser.
2. Determine what part of the wall needs to be washed. Sometimes it is a specific place (edges that people swing around, walls around light switches) and sometimes it is a specific thing that needs to be cleaned off (pencil, food, crayon, permanent marker, boogers, poop).
3. Using the spray bottle, moisten the wall. If there is a waterfall of drips cascading down the wall, you sprayed too much. Use a little less next time. Scrub the area that needs scrubbed. If you think it is still dirty, keep scrubbing. If you think a parent can tell that it is still dirty, keep scrubbing. Those are not necessarily the same things.
4. If you are scrubbing so hard that the paint is coming off, you are doing a thorough job but you need to stop. Be a little more gentle, please.
5. Put your cleaning things away.

Bedtime

Ah, bedtime. Every parent's nightmare. Why is it that we can ask the children to do the same activity every night at the same time for years and they still look at us with questioning eyes, wondering, "What do you mean brush my teeth? What strange language are you using?"

On the bright side, bedtime can be a very relaxing, calming, connecting time of day. I have one child in particular that has claimed bedtime as his snuggle time with me - and won't do it any other time of day. It is his time away from everyone else, and he takes advantage of the opportunity to really open up to me. As tired as I may be, I wouldn't miss that connection for the world.

"Get in PJs."

This means:

1. Go to the bedroom.
2. Take off dirty clothes.
3. Put on pajamas.
4. Take care of what you just took off (see "getting changed").
5. Note that this instruction does NOT mean "get a Calvin and Hobbes comic book and read on your bed." It also does not mean "start playing a game," "finish the art project you started three days ago," "fight with your sibling," or "time to start your homework that is due tomorrow."

"Brush teeth."

This means:

1. Go to the bathroom. Do not pass go, do not collect $200, do not cut your toenails or make an origami ninja star. Go directly to the bathroom.

2. Floss. You only need about 8-10 inches. The entire roll of floss will not ensure a better flossing job. When you are done, throw the used floss in the trash. It does not belong on the counter, on the floor, or back in the drawer. While I appreciate that you're trying to be economical, you do not need to reuse the floss. Yuck.

3. Touching only your own toothbrush and the toothpaste, apply toothpaste to your toothbrush only. If you spill any toothpaste, clean it up now.

4. Brush for at least two minutes. Longer is good. Get all the sides of your mouth. Front and back, top and bottom. Incisors, canines, premolars, and molars. Lots of good brushing.

5. Spit in the sink. Not on the counter, or a sibling, on the floor, or down your shirt. In the sink.

6. Rinse toothbrush and the sink where you spit, and put your toothbrush away.

7. If in the process of following steps 3-6 your toothbrush teleported to the floor, the bathtub, or the toilet, it needs to be washed (floor or tub) or disposed of (toilet). See me if you are not sure what to do with the dirty toothbrush, but please do not use it to brush your teeth if it went in the toilet.

8. OPTIONAL BUT RECOMMENDED: Pee. See "Peeing." But not while brushing.

Congratulations! After getting in pajamas and brushing your teeth, you're ready for bed. You may go read quietly in bed or on a cushion in the playroom while you wait for devotional. This should happen immediately after "Get in PJs" and "Brush teeth."

Bedtime is your job. Don't impede others from doing their job. If a room is occupied, find something peaceful and non-annoying to do for two minutes, and check the room again. Repeat until the space you want becomes available.

Devotional

1. This is our family's time to share and be vulnerable. Please show respect by sitting peacefully (see "Sitting") and listening respectfully. Reading your own material right now is inappropriate.
2. Manage your after school and evening time so you can participate. Devotional > homework. You had lots of time to do it. Devotional > drink of water. It can wait. Devotional > dinner chores. You'll have to finish in the morning. I will make sure to wake you up so you have plenty of time.

For more on our family's devotional, please see the appendix in the back. It is my favorite part of our family's culture.

Going to sleep

Parents see this as the natural next step after the previous steps are completed. For some reason, children don't.
1. Get in bed.
2. Close your eyes.
3. Don't open them again until morning.

This is not a difficult process. I don't understand why the process usually looks like this:
1. Get in bed.
2. Get out of bed to adjust something on the dresser.
3. Get in bed.
4. Get out of bed to get one more hug.
5. Get in bed.
6. Get out of bed to ask for a drink.
7. Drink the water.
8. Get in bed.
9. Get out of bed to turn the light off.
10. Get in bed.
11. Close eyes.
12. Open eyes.
13. Get out of bed to use the bathroom.
14. Get in bed.
15. Get out of bed to get a stuffed animal.
16. Get in bed with the stuffed animal.
17. Get out of bed to get another stuffed animal.
18. And so on.
I just don't get it.

School

At this point in time, all our children are in public school. We have homeschooled in the past and appreciate this option for families. We are lucky to live in a community where there are a variety of educational options, and have chosen to go the public school route for now.

Getting ready for school

1. Get out of bed with enough time to do tasks 2-6.
2. Go to the bathroom if you need to. See "Peeing" and "Pooping" for instructions.
3. Get dressed. See "Getting changed" for instructions.
4. Do something to make your hair look how you want it. As long as it is clean-ish and not in tangles, it will pass parental inspection. If you can't figure out how to do this with longer hair, we will make sure that it is kept at a length that requires less maintenance.
5. Eat breakfast. See "kitchen" section for instructions.
6. Decide: school lunch or home lunch? Pack if necessary. See "lunch-making" for instructions.
7. Get out the door before the bus comes and put your shoes on. If you choose not to wear socks in your shoes, you may have blisters by the end of the day. Yes, you will still have to participate in PE with blisters. Please wear socks next time.

Homework

1. Do it. Before dinner if possible. Before games, or leisure reading. If you need a snack, or to let off steam after school, that is fine. Homework should be started within 45 minutes of getting home from school.
2. UNLESS you are on cooking duty for the evening. Then homework needs to be done sooner.
3. Whatever you get out to use for your homework, put it away when you're done.

The explosion that is school stuff when you come home

- Put your backpack in its place. In our house, this is your locker if it fits, or out of the way in the office if your backpack is too wide for your locker. If you go to a friend's house after school, please ask where you can put it. Don't leave it in the middle of their entryway.
- Your coat goes in your locker or gets hung up in the closet.
- If you took anything out of your backpack that needs to go back in it, put it there.
- If you took anything out of your backpack that does not need to go back in it, put it where it belongs. School papers can go to a parent.
- Lunches: If you didn't finish your lunch at school, please do so for your afternoon snack. When you're done, either wash the container or put it in the dishwasher. Your lunch bag gets put away, not left on the counter or in the middle of the floor.

Out and about

This is one thing that has definitely gotten easier since having babies and toddlers. I remember shortly after my first child was born taking 45 minutes to get out the door: Make sure that we won't be out during naptime. Or feeding time. Make sure the diaper bag is packed. Feed baby. Burp baby. Change diaper. Put my own shoes on. Change the baby's clothes because he spit up on them. Put another change of clothes in the diaper bag, just in case. Put a change of clothes for me in the diaper bag. Change diaper again. It was a miracle I went anywhere.

Now that my kids are older, the challenges are different, but I am grateful for the independence that growing up brings.

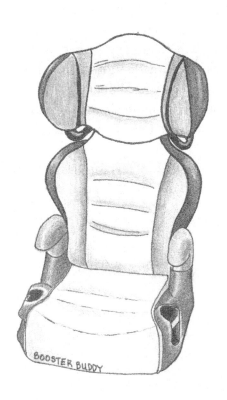

Riding in the car, part I

1. Open the door to the vehicle.
2. If you ride in a booster or child's car seat, get into the spot where your seat already is. This simplifies step three.
3. If you don't ride in a booster or child's seat, choose an available seat to land in. If someone is already in the seat you wanted, you can refer to the section on "sitting" or "saying please." If neither of those options work, you will need to find another seat. Standing outside the car throwing a fit about someone being in your seat will not get us to our destination more quickly, and when you are in a hurry because it is your best friend's birthday party and we're already running 20 minutes late and you're sure you're going to miss the best part of the party and your brother is standing outside the car screaming because you're in his seat and he just can't get in the car unless he gets that seat..... I'll ask you if you remember the time you stood outside the car pouting.
4. Sit in your seat with your bottom on the seat.
5. Put your seatbelt on the way it was designed to be worn.
6. Once the car has started moving, keep your seatbelt buckled and worn properly. Again, it takes longer to get to our destination when I have to stop the car every 30 feet because someone keeps unbuckling his or her seatbelt.

Hold on to your hats, we're not there yet!

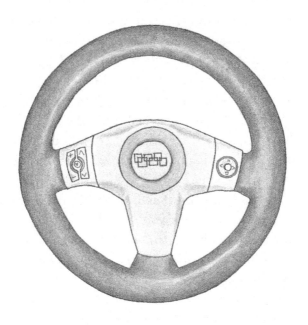

Riding in the car, part II

7. Keep all body parts and things coming from your body (air, projectiles, etc) in your own space.
8. If you are sitting next to someone who insists on sharing his or her exhaled air with you, please be comforted in the fact that 16% of the air they breathe out is oxygen. You will not suffocate.
9. When we reach our destination, if you are in the rear seat, wait for the people in the middle seats to get out. Then, move the seat forward. Please do not climb over the seat onto someone's head in order to get out of the car unless it is an absolute emergency. Wanting a drink of water first does not qualify as an emergency.

Welcome
to the
Misty
mountain
Lodge

- menu -

Appetizers
Lembas Bread
Mushroom Toast
Mini Quiche
Hobbit Hash

Entrees
Hearty Stew
Roast Mutton
Fish & Chips
Cottage Pie
Roasted Chicken
Spiced Beef

Desserts
Tea Cake
Blackberry Tart
Ring Cookies
Apple Pie & Cream

Drinks
Mirwvor
Tea
Toasted Mallow
Grog
Ent Draught

- menu -

At a restaurant

1. See "eating." All of it applies here. We practice good manners at home so you know how to use them when we're at a restaurant or you're eating at a friend's house. You are expected to use those good manners when we go out.
2. Recognize that not everyone in the restaurant wants to hear what you have to say. Keep your voice at a reasonable level.
3. The goal of eating out is *not* to get kicked out of the restaurant. Dumping sugar packets on the table, shooting straw wrappers across the room, playing tag, and throwing napkin paper airplanes are all unacceptable behaviors. Even if your grandmother is setting the example by doing any of the above.

In the store

- Most of the time, if you ask for something, you won't get it. You're better off asking, "Did you remember to put _____ on your list?" I'll probably still say that we're not getting it, but your odds are better if you ask that way.
- If you whine about not getting something, you definitely won't get it.
- Throwing a full-on tantrum means we leave the store and don't come back in. And you don't come with me the next time I go to the store.
- Shoplifting things will result in a trip back to the store so you can return the item to the store manager and apologize in person. If the item was already eaten/thrown away/used, you will pay for the item along with the apology.

Going out with friends or to a friend's house

1. Check in with me first. I want to know where you are because I care about you.

2. If I ask you to come by a certain time, it is for a reason. Whether it is for dinner, bedtime, a family event, or just because I know you'll need some downtime, I need you to respect that time because it shows that I can trust you. Ignoring it will result in reduced freedom for you until you can rebuild trust.

3. If your friends are making poor choices in their lives, let's have a chat. If you have a friend who is into drugs, I don't want you at their house unsupervised, but they are welcome here (drug-free).

4. For expectations at your friend's house, please see "With friends or extended family."

With friends or extended family

1. Best manners.
2. Be kind.
3. Don't die.

(Yes, this is what we actually say to each other when going to a friend's house)

Outside chores

Our family lives on a small farm in Washington state. As parents, we feel it is important for our kids to have meaningful responsibilities, and have had different chores over the years for our kids to be in charge of. Some of these jobs have included feeding dogs, cats, geese, chickens, ducks, and sheep, yard cleanup, mowing, planting, and weeding. We have high expectations for our kids to help, but also recognize that play is a huge part of childhood. Please be assured that they have plenty of time for recreation, and not all of their time is spent working.

Morning birds expectations

1. Feed and water the chickens in the front coop
2. Feed and water the chickens in the back coop.
3. Let the geese out.
4. If it rained overnight, yes, you still have to give the birds water. Drops of rainwater are not enough to survive on.

Evening birds expectations

1. Repeat morning birds, but put the geese away in their coop instead of letting them out.
2. Move the chicken tractors to fresh ground.
3. If there are eggs to collect, do it, and gently remind the person whose job it is to wash eggs that they need to do it. Leaving them on the front porch for the raccoons to eat overnight means a big mess to clean up the next morning, and yes, you will all have to help.
4. If you use the rest of a feed bag, empty the dregs into a new bag and put the old bag in the trash.
5. If you spill feed, clean it up. Please don't expect the mice to do it for you, because they leave poop behind and that is less fun to clean up.

Cleaning the porch

1. Put all the shoes on the racks. Yes, I know, people are supposed to do this when they take their shoes off. When is the last time you put your shoes on the rack when you took them off?
2. If there is anything else that does not belong on the porch, please put it in the appropriate place. Dirty washcloths go in the laundry. Pens and paper go with the art supplies. Toothbrushes go in the trash. (Do not tell your sister it is her new toothbrush!) Tools get put away. If you can't tell what it is, it goes in the trash.
3. Sweep all the dirt off the porch. Not into Dad's shoe. Even if you think it is funny, he doesn't.

Getting the mail

1. Walk down to the mailbox.
2. Open the mailbox.
3. If there is anything inside, take it out.
4. Bring the mail up to the house. Leaving a trail of mail up the driveway is not an effective way of accomplishing this.
5. If there is mail for you, you may open it. If it says, "To the parent/guardian of (your name)," it is not for you, it is for a parent. So don't open it.
6. Give all the mail to a parent. The mail should not have to be a treasure hunt for us.

Outside activities

Note: This includes but is not limited to bikes, tools, helmets, shovels, games, random sticks that need to be saved in a special place because "it's my favorite stick!", etc.

- If you get it out, play with it, see it, trip over it, or otherwise notice that something needs to be put away, just do it. Even if it isn't yours. But especially if you were the one who got it out.

Planting things

1. Dig a hole the appropriate size for the thing you're planting. If it is a lettuce seedling, the hole needs to be small. If it is a tree, the hole needs to be bigger than the size of the pot the tree is currently in.
2. Put one plant in each hole. Yes, it initially gets the job done faster to put all the swiss chard plants in one big hole, but you'll have to go back and do it again. And that takes longer.
3. Cover the roots with dirt. If you can see the roots, the plant is not actually planted.
4. Don't cover the plant with dirt. If you can't see the green part of the plant, it is generally too deep.
5. Water it. Gently. Washing it away is bad for plant health.

Weeding the garden

1. You can choose to wear gloves, or not. I suggest gloves.
2. You can choose to wear play/work clothes or not. But when you wear your favorite shirt and it gets stained and you can't wear it to school anymore, this is not my fault.
3. Pull up weeds out of the garden. Not the newly planted seedlings. If you're not sure which plants are weeds and which are not, please ask. Sometimes the weeds are right next to the veggies or flower plants, and when you pull up the weed, it pulls the other plant up with it. Two options: gently hold the other plant in place while you pull the weed out, or pull them both out, separate the keeper, and replant it (not the weed). See "planting things."
4. If you leave the roots of the weeds in the ground, you will have to do the job again in a few days.
5. If you leave the weeded plants on top of the plants we want in the garden, it will smother and kill the plants we want. If you smother the watermelon seedling, we don't have a watermelon plant. No watermelon for you.
6. Please put the weeds in the compost (plants that have not gone to seed yet) or the trash (plants that have already gone to seed).

Mowing the lawn

Note: This chore is very similar to vacuuming, but with the added excitement of sharp spinning things and the possibility of losing a limb.

1. Before beginning, make sure that all obstacles are removed from the area to be mowed, including frisbees, cones, all types of balls, large sticks, shoes, coats, hoses, tools, dishes, and smart phones.
2. Start the mower.
3. Using parallel paths, mow up and down the lawn. Artistic creativity does not earn bonus points here, though I have seen very nice paisley patterns in our lawn before.
4. When you're done, inspect your work. Are there patches of tall grass? Please go back and mow them.
5. Put the lawnmower away.

Recreation

I know, it is shocking that with all these rules and responsibilities my kids still have time to play, but they have plenty of down time. I couldn't just let them play without some kind of restrictions, so I came up with rules for that, too.

Playing a game

1. Make sure everyone who is playing actually wants to play. A person who has been coerced into playing will probably either a) leave partway through the game or b) cheat, like they did last time they didn't really want to play. Then you end up unhappy. So save yourself the unhappiness.
2. Make sure everyone knows the rules. It is not cheating if you're playing a version of checkers where you can go on the red spaces, as long as everyone is playing by the same rules. It *is* cheating to change the rules in the middle of the game to your advantage, or to "forget" to explain a rule to someone until they break it.
3. When your game is over, clean it up. Everyone who played at some point during the game should help clean it up.
4. Put it back on the shelf where it goes.

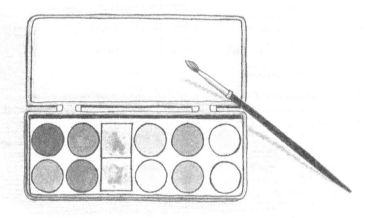

Using art supplies

- If you get something out, put it away.
- If something falls on the floor, breaks, becomes empty, falls down the heating vent, jumps out the window, spills, or runs away, just take care of it. You could pick it up, throw it away, refill it, get it out of the heating vent, pick it up from outside the window, wipe or vacuum it up, or catch it.
- If you take something out of the area where you're working, put it away when you're done with it. It won't come back on its own.
- If you find something that might need to be put with the art supplies when you're walking around the house, pick it up and put it away.

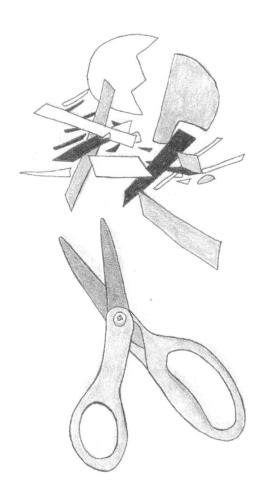

Toys, hobbies, and other sundries:

Note: This includes but is not limited to: games, books, musical instruments, pencils, clipboards, cards, pillows, blankets, stuffed animals, socks, Rubik's cubes, flashlights, flyswatters, scissors, paper, tiny scraps of paper cut up by scissors....

- Put it away when you're done with it. Away does not mean on the back of the couch, under the couch, under the table, on the floor, on a chair, over or inside the heating vent, or out the window. It means put away.

Climbing trees

1. Choose a tree that is big enough to support you. Climbing the four foot tall heirloom apple tree we planted last year not only won't get you very high up, it will also get you in trouble.
2. Choose branches that are big enough and solid enough to support you.
3. If you have the confidence and skills to climb up the tree, you have the confidence and skills to climb down, too.

Hiking with toddlers/preschoolers/elementary aged kids

- Stay on the trail.
- Stay where we can see you.
- Don't eat anything you pick unless it is first approved by an adult.

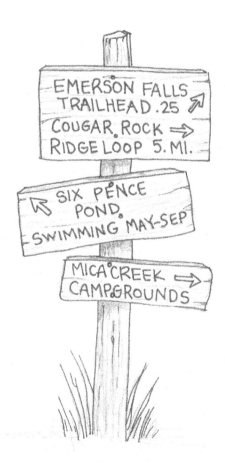

Hiking with upper elementary/middle/high school kids

- Don't be stupid. Going off trail in a fragile ecosystem is damaging. Going off trail to cut corners is rude and causes erosion. Going off trail to a specific destination you're navigating to can be empowering.
- Stay in a group. As a parent, I want to be able to hear you if there is not an adult in your group. If there is a responsible teenager/adult in your group and you've communicated with me what your plan is for meeting up again, you may go ahead on the trail.
- Stop and wait for the entire group at all trail intersections.

Biking

- Wear a helmet.
- Don't be stupid. The cars are bigger than you. And the ground is harder than you think.
- If you are riding farther than the end of the driveway, you need to check in with me before you go so I know where you are headed, who you are with, and when you plan on being back. This is because I care about you, not because I am trying to ruin your life.
- Bikes at our house are community property. While you may have a preferred bike, if a sibling is currently using it, you may not push them off it so you can use 'your' bike. Use your words to communicate. See "Conflict resolution."

Playing golf

1. Find a ball. Any size will do.
2. Find a long narrow object. Golf clubs work well, as do baseball bats, sticks, PVC pipes, and umbrellas.
3. Find a target. A series of targets is great, but if you only have one, that will do. Trees are good, but narrow. Rose bushes are easier to hit, but harder to remove the ball from. Breakable things should be avoided. Digging a hole might be a possibility, but check with an adult first. People are not good targets, even if it is your little brother and he is willing to be the target.
4. Place your ball at least 20 feet in front of any breakable object, including car windows, house windows, neighbor's windows, stained glass windows.... Maybe this whole golf thing is a bad idea in the first place.
5. Aiming for the target (not the windows behind you), hit the ball with the long narrow object. First person to hit the target with the ball wins. Breaking a window (or any other valuable object) will likely result in disqualification and an immediate end to the game.

Media

When people look back on this time in history, I believe that they will remember this time as the age of information. We are surrounded by media everywhere we turn, in all its forms. Selecting what comes into our minds and our homes is a major undertaking that our family chooses to do with intention. I value the experience of real, physical, tactile life, and encourage my kids to participate in 'analog' activities and to minimize their digital screen time.

School night screen time

1. School work, including homework and instrument practicing must be done.
2. Personal cleanup must be done (room tidy, school stuff away, etc)
3. Completing the following activities qualifies you for screen time (but does not ensure that you get it):
   a. 30+ minutes physical activity
   b. 30+ minutes outside time
   c. 30+ minutes of reading
   d. 30+ minutes of play, such as a game, making art, practicing your hobby, or toys
4. Dinner cleanup and chores must be done
5. 15 minutes of informational/communication screen time is OK
6. Devices get turned off at 7:45

My kids have asked if running outside for 30 minutes can count as physical activity, outside time, and hobby time. No, it doesn't. But I will count it for two things at a time. Now go play.

Weekend/vacation screen time

1. If it is not raining, go outside. If the weather is nice, take advantage of it - no screen time today. (This was my kids' idea, not mine!)
2. Chores and homework must be done.
3. 30+ minutes of physical activity
4. 60+ minutes outside time
5. 30+ minutes of reading
6. 60+ minutes of play - some examples: game, art, hobby, toys
7. 15 minutes of recreational or learning screen time if the weather is bad

What! You only let your kids have 15 minutes of screen time?! Yes. And we watch movies and do other screen time activities as a family. We put on music they want as long as it is not offensive. We enforce the 15 minutes limit, but recognize that they are exposed to screen time as my husband and I get work done on the computer, as siblings watch educational videos for school, and as kids on the school bus play games to pass this time. My children are not deprived, nor are they social outcasts. They are familiar with the latest video games, songs, and trends even though they don't participate in them at home.

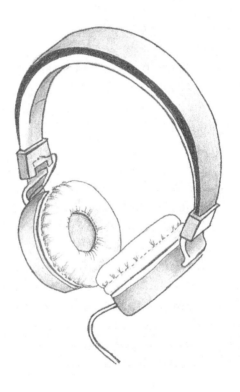

Music

1. You may listen to any genre of music you would like. However, if it has inappropriate language or content, it may be vetoed and you'll need to find something else to listen to.
2. If your music is disturbing others because of volume or age-inappropriate content, you need to either
   a. Turn it off
   b. Put headphones on
3. If your behavior is negatively affected by the music you are listening to, you will lose listening privileges. For example:
   a. Singing "Frozen" ALL THE TIME
   b. Using unkind or inappropriate language that you learned from music
   c. Physical violence toward someone while listening to your music
4. If you ever play "It's a Small World After All," you will be banned from music for life.

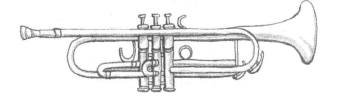

Musical instruments

1. Learning an instrument is something that is valued in our home, and I appreciate that you are putting forth the time, effort, and work it takes to master something hard.
2. However, the time to learn an instrument is not:
   a. During a meal
   b. At bedtime
   c. When someone else is already practicing
   d. When anyone in the house is asleep or trying to go to sleep
   e. When someone is on the phone
   f. When someone is trying to focus on homework in the room where you started practicing after they asked you to be quiet
   g. Right outside the door of the room where someone is trying to focus on homework where you started practicing after they asked you to be quiet
3. Please be respectful of other people's need for quiet time.

Reading a book

1. Choose the book you would like to read. If someone else is currently reading it, you will need to choose something else or ask politely if you can read it. See "saying please." This should avoid your having to look up "Conflict resolution."

2. Find a comfortable place to read. If someone is occupying the place where you would like to be, find a different place. See "sitting."

3. Read! Usually, this means in your own head. For those of you who feel compelled to read out loud every time you read a book, your comfortable place should be a comfortable place behind a closed door with no one else in the room.

4. When you're done reading, please put the book away on the bookshelf. Not on the couch, not on the windowsill closest to the couch, not on the bench 18 inches from the bookshelf you pulled the book from, not on the stairs, and not in the middle of the floor.

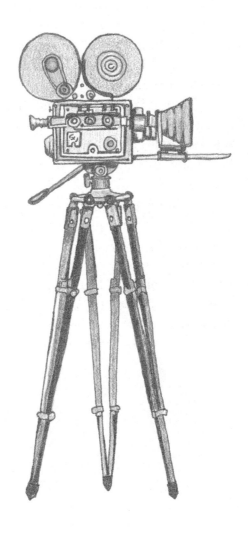

Movies

- Choose a movie appropriate for the most sensitive member of the group. If that is Mom, or the youngest person, or the most easily scared, please respect that and choose something everyone can watch.
- You're in charge of your own choices at other people's homes. You know yourself better than anyone else; stick up for yourself and your preferences.

Getting along with other people

Choose kindness. Every time.

House Rules

How we got here

Now that you've read how we do things now, maybe some of you would like the back story. Why do we do the things we do? What are our current motivations? Why do we make the effort to wash our own poop off of cut up flannel sheets?

This, my friends, is the rest of the story.

On childrearing in general

I am guessing that many parents could write their own book on how they raise kids and why they do it that way.

First of all, I am not a parenting expert. I've read a lot of books, most other adults I meet like my kids, and I like my own kids (at least most of the time). Those are the only qualifications I have on giving any parenting advice.

Second, my parenting philosophies and strategies change as I learn things, as my kids get older, as our family situation changes, and they are dependent on the child I am dealing with at the time. I love that each of my children are unique, and to try to parent them identically would not meet their individual or developmental needs.

I have tried to go with an adaptive but firm approach to parenting - meet the child where they are at, but don't compromise the values you're trying to teach them. Sounds simple, but complicated to do in practice.

When my kids were relatively young (8 and under), I did a lot of soul searching about what values I really wanted them to internalize before they left home. I settled on peace, love, respect, and integrity. It is upon those four values that I base my parenting. Your family may value totally different things, but when I discipline, when I correct misbehavior, when I teach, when I help resolve conflict, I try to base my response and my correction on those values.

On why we make our kids do chores in the first place, why they don't get paid, and how they can earn money

I am a true believer in teaching kids independence and responsibility. From the time they were able, our kids have been expected to help out. When they were tiny, that meant picking up toys and helping move laundry from the washer to the dryer. As they get older, my expectations of them grow, too.

I want my kids to launch into the adult world with an arsenal of skills that will allow them to become successful humans, and I believe that teaching them independence is a big part of that. To me, knowing how to complete household tasks (including fixing things) and being independent in the kitchen are a big part of that.

My partner and I have talked a lot about different compensation systems for chores: allowance, being paid by the chore, complicated reimbursement systems, etc. Though we've tried some, at this point in our lives I believe that there are many things that you do just because you're part of the family. Laundry, dishes, cleaning up after yourself, helping clean the bathrooms - they are all part of a functioning household, and I expect that everyone will participate in some way to accomplish those tasks, without compensation.

Our kids don't earn money for extra jobs either, because we want them to recognize that you have to do hard things just because they need to be done, not because there is a reward at the end.

Our kids can start earning money for household chores after they complete their "13 Project." Since we are not involved with a religion that celebrates coming of age, we wanted to do something as a family to recognize the beginning of the transition into adulthood. The 13 Project is given to a child when they turn 13 years old; after they complete 13 tasks (some assigned by parents, some independently chosen), they can start earning money for the jobs they do around the house.

The 13 project includes nine required tasks:
- Plan and cook 13 full meals independently
- With $13 to spend, use a map to navigate from one place to another and buy a gift for a friend and a gift for a homeless person.

- Plan a party for 13 people using a budget of $30
- Write 13 thank you letters to people who have influenced you
- Be able to fix 13 things (parents' choice)
- Interview 13 adults about what it means to be an adult
- Perform 13 hours of community service
- Plan 13 dates
- Work up to 13 minutes of meditation/other form of spiritual practice

And four of the child's choice of the following:
- Research 13 hobbies you're interested in pursuing
- Plan and execute a 13 mile overnight backpacking trip
- Read 13 books (parents' choice) and write about why it is an important book
- Complete a 13 item scavenger hunt in a big city using public transportation
- Plan and execute a 13 mile bike ride
- Build a 30 second timer with at least 13 parts
- Complete an art project about what it means to be an adult
- Grow 13 pounds of produce in your own garden
- Make a playlist of 13 songs that define you
- ???? (they can come up with their own, too, to be approved by Mom or Dad)

After completing 13 tasks, we have a big celebration, invite all their friends, and welcome our child into adulthood. From then on, they not only can earn money for their contributions to household chores, but they also have increased financial responsibilities, such as paying for their own clothes, recurring payments (media or phone subscriptions), and any 'extra' things they want (birthday presents for friends, outings that cost money, etc).

We also encourage our kids to appropriately work outside the home. That may mean running a lemonade stand, walking the neighbor's dog, serving at a fast food restaurant, or working at a summer recreational job.

On picking battles

"I can't believe you don't make your kids make their beds!" "You let your child go out in public wearing *that*?" "Isn't it time for a haircut for _____?"

As a parent, I found that I have to balance prioritizing my values with teaching autonomy. I am learning that some things that parents hold as sacred cows, I don't really care about. For me, it comes down to prioritizing what our family values are and how those are expressed.

For example, I am much more lenient on clothing choices than some parents. I know some parents will lay clothes out for their children the day before school so they know their child is wearing a decent-looking outfit. That is all fine and good, and their children are much better dressed than mine.

However, as long as the clothing my kids wear shows respect for reasonable school rules (covering certain body parts and no inappropriate words or advertising) and shows appreciation for their education and their teacher's time (no visible stains or holes), I don't care what they wear. I entered the realm of public school expecting that my kids would wear collared shirts on a regular basis, looking nice every day with their hair neatly combed. What turned out was that my kids wanted to be comfortable and express themselves. I am OK with that. Even if that means seeing a child wear a tye-dye shirt with plaid shorts and neon knee-high socks to middle school.

I often ask myself the question, "Is the lesson I want my kids to learn worth the battle I am going to inevitably fight with them?" Sometimes it is, and sometimes it isn't. I don't need to battle with my kids for control; I will battle with my kids if their behavior conflicts with our family's values.

On toilet cloths, the environment, and our house

How are these three things related, you ask? Great question. I'll get there.

We have used toilet cloths instead of toilet paper for about seven years, as of the writing of the book. Our initial reasons for using toilet cloths were:

1. Cost. Invest in $8 worth of secondhand flannel sheets, cut them into 8-10" squares, and you have a year's supply of toilet paper.

2. Environment. No more virgin forests being cut down so we can wipe our rear ends.

Since then, we've realized a few other benefits in addition to our original reasons:

1. We have cleaning rags available anytime. They are more durable than paper towels and we have a system for storing the nasty ones until we can wash them. We have essentially stopped using paper towels. I buy a roll once a year, maybe.
2. They make great handkerchiefs. They're really soft and travel well.
3. They feel really nice to use when you're done going to the bathroom.
4. They do a better job cleaning my skin than paper, and I can moisten the rag in the sink for an especially cleansing experience.

While not a perfect environmental solution (it still uses energy, water, and soap to wash the cloths regularly), I feel good about the choice we have made.

Using toilet cloths exemplifies that we try to live our lives in a sustainable, intentional way. We minimize one use plastics, we use non-toxic cleaners, we drive an electric car or use alternative transportation whenever possible, we use a chainmail stainless steel washcloth in the kitchen, we compost food waste, and we buy most things secondhand. We're not perfect, but we try to minimize our negative environmental impact.

When we built a house in 2017, we extended those principles to the new home. We built it to be extremely energy efficient, took advantage of passive solar energy, added solar panels and used reclaimed or sustainable materials wherever it was financially feasible. Our goal was net zero (producing as much energy as we would use, balanced over the course of a year); we have not reached our goal yet, but we are working on it.

In order to find reclaimed materials for the house, we scoured Craigslist on a regular basis. We also regularly visited the local Habitat for Humanity ReStore, as well as The Rebuilding Center, a local reclaimed building materials store. Through our searching, we ended up finding much of the interior finish material that we needed: reclaimed slate tile flooring; gym flooring from Reed College; interior doors from a 1920's craftsman home; used kitchen cabinets that fit our layout; 1x12 planks that we used for shelving and baseboards from 100-year-old house being deconstructed. We also used a collection of old maps as flooring for some areas, glueing them to the floor and coating them with polyurethane. Using reclaimed materials has made for a fun, quirky, unique home for our family.

Finding sustainable materials locally has also built human connection. I found the maps we used for our flooring on Craigslist; the gentleman getting rid of the maps was cleaning out his late father's home and found three boxes of topographic (and other) maps. When he found out we were using them as flooring, he was really excited. "My dad would have loved that," he told us.

We did make compromises on our material choices. We really wanted to incorporate either clay flooring or clay walls into our new home; however, after looking at the time we had, the logistics of supporting a heavy floor or wall, and the expense of using those materials, we decided to use more conventional materials. We also used new (instead of reclaimed) lumber for the structure of our house, new metal roofing, cement fiber siding, and new drywall on the walls. While a part of me wishes we had been able to build a strawbale house, or use lath and plaster for our interior walls, or find reclaimed, not leaky metal roofing, the other part of me recognizes that we all just do our best at the time, and that has to be OK.

Overall, sustainable living and being conscious of our environmental impact guide many of our daily decisions - from toilet paper to building materials!

On food and cooking

The kitchen is the hub in our home. A few years ago, we settled on a small farm so we could grow more of our own food and teach our kids about where their food comes from. We started out growing vegetables to sell at farmer's markets, but now just grow food in a smaller garden for our own use. We by no means grow all the food we need, but we have big dreams and do what we can now to preserve our food to last throughout the year.

Diet is such a touchy subject. My partner teaches health at a community college, and has a background in exercise and nutrition. While there are lots of fads out there - many of them healthy (but not all) - we try to keep food simple. Our philosophy aligns with Michael Pollan's: Eat food. Not too much. Mostly Plants. We eat dinner together whenever we can, we involve our kids in the planning, preparation, and cleanup, and we try to do it on a budget.

We cook mostly from scratch, but we pick and choose the prepared foods that make our lives easier. We've decided that dried pasta, canned tomatoes, and bagels (for example) are all worth the processing, time and energy other people put into them. We try to minimize processed foods to things we can read the ingredients for, and that are time or cost prohibitive to do on our own. When we have time and it isn't blazing hot outside, we try to bake our own bread, and we home-can the surplus food from our garden.

Something we could do better on is buying locally. We have many friends that farm, but feeding a family of seven on organic, local food would blow our budget. We support local farmers when we can, and that doesn't always mean buying produce from them. We have volunteered as a family on their farms, helped with marketing, and watched their kids so they can get farm work done.

I also think it is really important to get kids into the kitchen to help - not just with cleaning up, but with prep and cooking, too. My experience is that most kids LOVE to be a part of this. We have tried different rotations and ways to involve our kids in this process. I love the idea that we can change systems over time and to meet the needs of our family at any particular stage in life. The way we currently rotate meal prep is that each child has a full week of helping cook. They don't have after-meal kitchen cleanup responsibilities that week, and they are responsible for planning the week's meals on Sunday so I (or we) can get the necessary ingredients.

This has had some great results. I love that my kids are taking ownership of the meals they are cooking, and at the same time learning planning, purchasing, prepping, and cooking skills. It has enabled us to get out of the rut we usually found ourselves in (pasta one of three ways, bean burritos, and veggies on rice, repeat). I find that my kids (for the most part) are more willing to try a new food if they have invested in the preparation of it.

We have chosen not to have a microwave in our home, which both complicates and simplifies things. Reheating leftovers is a little more complicated, and it takes planning ahead if we want to use something from the freezer for dinner. However, it also encourages us to not eat processed or convenience foods, as they are less convenient when it takes 30 minutes to cook in the oven.

Snacks at our house are usually fruits, vegetables, or leftovers. We don't really keep traditional "snack" food at our house (chips, crackers, candy, microwave popcorn, granola bars, etc). If my kids want a snack, they can grab fresh fruit, dried fruit, veggies, or leftovers.

On money and frugality

Like most young students, both my husband and I experienced the pinch of having little money during college both before and after we were married. We minimized expenses whenever we could, from not going out to eat to using cloth diapers. We did our best to avoid monthly expenses (subscriptions or automatic payments), and went without many extras.

As our family has grown, so have our expenses. We still try to minimize expenses through a variety of methods:
- We rarely go out to eat.
- We still try not to have monthly payments other than basic utilities. We do have internet, internet phone ($5/month) and a cell phone bill, which is talk/text only with no data. We don't subscribe to TV, magazines, monthly "send me things" (like razors, sponges, or cleaning products) or online media (Netflix, Hulu, etc).
- We eat mostly vegetarian, avoid processed foods, and buy in bulk, which cuts down on our grocery bill. I use coupons for the things we need but don't buy things we don't. I usually buy generic instead of name brand.
- We don't smoke or consume alcohol.
- We combine trips to save money on gas and wear and tear on vehicles.

- We try to purchase everything we can secondhand through thrift stores, ebay, or online classifieds. If we do buy something new, we do the research to get the best value for our money.
- We conserve energy at home to lower our electric bill.
- We lean toward a DIY lifestyle, fixing and repairing things whenever possible and on our own.

Some people think of it as deprivation; however, living the way we do allows us to save money on a limited income and pay cash for large purposes. We don't subscribe to any popular philosophy on budgeting or finance - we spend less than we make, we keep money in savings, and we save up so we can pay cash for large purposes.

We do use a credit card, but pay it off every month, benefiting from 1% back and not ever paying interest. We keep our money at a credit union where it earns 2.5% interest every month. Our only debt is our mortgage.

Another big influence on my financial and lifestyle perspective is the time that I spent in Zimbabwe. I lived there for two months after I finished college classes. The trip was life-changing. Two things I learned are that wealth does not equal happiness, and that the typical idea of success in western culture is a limited viewpoint.

Because of this experience, rather than seeing "voluntary simplicity" as deprivation, I see it as a deeply satisfying lifestyle. It spills over from just being a wise way to live financially to fill the cup of a meaningful life that values time over money, experiences over stuff, and relationships over material goods.

On schooling

Other than politics and religion, it seems like schooling is one of the most divisive subjects a person can bring up in conversation. Homeschool, public school, or private school? Religious or secular curriculum? Classical education vs unschooling? Should schools teach values or leave that to the parents? What is the role of public school in the civil environment?

I am not here to answer these questions. I believe we live in a truly privileged society where many people have options about how to educate their children, and those decisions need to be left up to the parents to research and decide what is best for their child and their family at the time.

We started out homeschooling. It fit our lifestyle and our values, and I loved having the time with my kids and control over what they were learning. As my kids got older (and more numerous), it was more difficult, but still the right choice for our family.

In late 2010, we decided to move from Kentucky back to the Pacific Northwest. Having given birth to all our kids in different states (Colorado, Oregon, Utah, and Kentucky) shows we hadn't really settled down for more than two years in any location. We bought a 15 passenger van and a travel trailer, sold everything that didn't fit inside them, quit work, and left Kentucky.

The next year was a fun adventure, taught us a lot, and provided lots of family bonding opportunities. However, I felt strongly that once we settled down, the kids needed more stability and structure than I could provide in our temporary home of a travel trailer. We enrolled the two school-age kids in public school and stuck with that for a school year. The following year, I kept one of them home again, but since then, we have had all the kids in public school. I continue to reevaluate our family's situation every year and base the decision on what is best for each child and for our family as a whole.

I understand the arguments both for and against different schooling options. I love that we have the freedom to choose how we educate our children, and support parents' intentional decisions on how to do that.

On devotional

Our family has a wonderful tradition of having a family devotional (almost) every night. We have used this time to read various sacred books from religions around the world, discuss current events in the world or in our own family, explore poetry, read biographies of important people, discuss family policies, and talk about other important topics (ethics, friends, media, etc). We have discussed everything from meditation to how to have a conversation with a romantic interest, and from Martin Luther King Jr.'s influence on society to what to do if you have a friend talk about committing suicide.

I really appreciate this time as a family for a few reasons.

1. It allows us to have dedicated family time every night, all together.
2. It is a safe space (most of the time) to share vulnerable things.
3. It provides a structure for us (as parents) to discuss our values with our kids.
4. It gives the kids parent time without any distractions.

We usually gather after everyone is ready for bed. It is a nice transition from the busyness of the day to bedtime. We all sit in the same room and try to minimize distractions (i.e. no reading other books, working on homework, or playing with toys). Most of the time, we will read something from a library book, but I have purchased a few resources that are especially helpful or valuable to me, and we sometimes use Youtube or other online resources. After reading for a few minutes, we talk about what we have read and listen to hear our kids' thoughts on it, too. I really cherish this time to share and learn together.

We have also used this time to talk about tricky, sensitive, or awkward topics: consent, body image, appropriate touching, and healthy sexuality. Growing up in a conservative religion, I was taught clear lines about when not to have sex (ever! until you're married), but not much else. In my own family, I have tried to maintain an openness about these touchy subjects while still communicating my values.

On media

When my oldest child was six months old, I came to an abrupt realization about media. I can still picture our small, on-campus apartment with the TV in the corner. I was watching a show on HGTV while my son was playing on the floor, and realized I was paying more attention to the show than to my son. I got rid of the TV that weekend, and we haven't had one since. Not having a television has helped define our family culture and response to digital media in general.

Many families struggle with how to find an appropriate balance for their kids and screen time. I don't think screen time in itself is bad. There are many good, useful, fun apps and programs out there. My big concern at this point in our family is the things our children are missing out on when they are doing screen time. We talk about screen time and media a lot at our house, and I hope that our philosophy may be helpful for you.

In our home, people > devices. It is more important to interact with people than your device. If there are people around that want to do something with you, engage with them. If a friend is here, find something to do other than screen time (unless we're having a movie night). Meals are screen free so we can connect with each other face to face.

In addition to this, it looks like recent research is showing that shared screen time between parents and kids can help with relationship building. We watch an occasional movie all together and I am okay with the idea of connecting with my kids during screen time. The reality of the situation is that I can't sit with my kids every time they use a screen, so the bonding doesn't happen. If families find that this form of connection really builds relationships in their family, more power to them.

At our house, internet-based activities may only happen when a parent is home. We feel this is safest for our kids and allows us to continually have discussions about ads, content, appropriate social media engagement, and internet safety. Streaming music through a music app or already downloaded onto a device is fine, and downloaded ebooks/audiobooks are fine without adults around (until you violate our trust). Bedrooms and bathrooms are device-free zones. Bring a comic book in with you, but you don't need anything with a camera with you when you're sitting on the toilet.

We have tried having elaborate systems in place for "earning" screen time, including the system suggested in this book. I have found that I can't keep up with keeping track, and every system we have tried using ends up falling by the wayside eventually. Not only is it hard to monitor the details of everyone's time, but it really doesn't match with my philosophy of self-government. I want my kids to learn how to manage themselves, and that includes their media consumption.

Instead, we generally keep a 15 minute guideline for screen time. Homework that requires screen time is exempt from the 15 minute rule. My kids don't always get their 15 minutes, and they need to check in with me about how they want to use their time if they get it. I don't want to get too entrenched in the 15 minute limit, so that if I have a child who wants to learn to code, look up a recipe, digitally edit photographs, or use a tablet for artwork, they can do that. The screen isn't the bad guy, but it is an enticing distraction to real life if we're not intentional about how we use it.

As a parent, I keep in mind different purposes for screen use: recreational, informational, communication, and relationship building. At this point in our family, games, Youtube bingeing, social media, and shopping are recreational/entertainment screen activities for kids and may not happen during the week. If a child wants screen time during the school week, it is usually informational or learning screen time including learning apps (defined by parents), language learning, typing, moderated educational video sites, skill development videos, and finding audiobooks. Listening to music through Youtube is probably the most common screen use for my kids. Communication including email and messaging are important and we make time accommodations for that. As our children get older, social media may shift to this category.

The big picture for our family is that we want to focus on people and personal development. I want my kids to know how to choose their media intentionally, and to spend their lives doing what they *want* to do. Because of this, I encourage my kids to focus on "analog" time. If there is a physical alternative to the digital activity, I encourage my kids to do that instead. In our house, the screen is a tool to accomplish what we want to do with our lives rather than a taskmaster to dictate it.

Acknowledgements

Thanks to all those who listened, gave feedback, and proofread the book. Special thanks to Jessica Swanson for your incredible editing, Caren Hahn for her inspiration and counsel, and Karen Kennedy for planting the seed for publishing in the first place.

Thanks also to our families, for providing stories, examples, and patience throughout the process. We love you!

Garrett, there wouldn't be a family without you - thanks for being there through it all.

Alyssa Hoyt is a mother of five children who has a wide variety of interests. When she is not laughing with her kids, volunteering in the community or working on their small farm, you are likely to find her out on a hike, reading a book, or playing guitar.

Rachel Dietz is a self taught artist with a natural talent for creativity. She enjoys quality time with her husband and five children. She enjoys the outdoors and daily hikes through the majestic forests of Washington State. She loves family trips to Disneyland as well as embracing the Aloha spirit of the Hawaiian islands with her husband.

Made in the USA
Monee, IL
04 November 2020